THE TRYST

THE TRYST

AND OTHER POEMS

BY

LAUCHLAN MACLEAN WATT

AUTHOR OF

" BY STILL WATERS," " THE COMMUNION TABLE,"
" THE PREACHER'S LIFE AND WORK," " PRAYERS
FOR PUBLIC WORSHIP," ETC.

ALLENSON & CO. LTD.
7 RACQUET COURT, 114 FLEET ST.
LONDON, E.C.4

Printed in Great Britain by Ebenezer
Baylis & Son, Ltd., The Trinity Press,
Worcester, and London

TO

A BELOVED MEMORY

FOREWORD

WHEN *The Tryst* appeared in 1907 it received a
universal welcome, and went almost immediately
out of print. Ever since, inquiries regarding it
have been received, but various considerations
prevented a re-issue. The title poem and *The
Long Last Mile* made a very deep and lasting
impression, and are still continually asked for.
The former especially has been reprinted times
without number everywhere. The latter was the
constant comfort of the late Dr. F. B. Meyer,
during his last hours. This new edition, with
fresh poems, is issued in the hope that it may, like
its predecessor, find a place of its own in the heart
and by the pillow and in the lives of thinking men
and women.

CONTENTS

THE TRYST

O THE way sometimes is low,
  And the waters dark and deep,
And I stumble as I go.

But I have a tryst to keep:
  It was plighted long ago
With some who lie asleep.

And though days go dragging slow,
  And the sad hours gravewards creep,
And the world is hush'd with woe,

I neither wail nor weep,
  For He would not have it so:
And I have a tryst to keep.

THE LONG LAST MILE

CARRY me over the long last mile,
  Man of Nazareth, Christ for me!
Weary I wait by Death's dark stile,
    In the wild and the waste, where the wind
      blows free;
      And the shadows and sorrows come out of
        my past,
        Look keen through my heart,
        And will not depart,
Now that my poor world has come to its last!

Lord, is it long that my spirit must wait?
  Man of Nazareth, Christ for me!
Deep is the stream, and the night is late,
    And grief blinds my soul that I cannot see.
      Speak to me out of the silences, Lord,
        That my spirit may know
        As forward I go,
Thy pierc'd hands are lifting me over the ford!

CHRIST BY THE STREAM

THE river sang over the wave-worn stone,
   And down by the stream sat I;
And the bells of the village seem'd far and lone,
   When Christ came wandering by.

His hair was wet as the sea-drench'd sand,
   And His eyes like the waves were blue;
And I saw in the palm of His outstretch'd hand
   A nail-hole through and through.

"Dost thou fear to venture across the tide,
   For the water's eddy and roar?
O come to my shoulder, trembling child,
   And I will carry thee o'er."

But I saw, on His shoulder, a black bruise plain,
   And His side was rent and torn;
And I felt, on His brow, all scarr'd with pain,
   The prints of a crown of thorn.

"O why dost Thou come by our country stream,
   Thou Christ from heaven?" I said.
"Sweet are our fields, and the flowrets gleam,
   But the world sits by her dead."

He smiled as a man in a dream might smile,
   And He answered low to me—
"When I walk atween these meadows green,
   I remember Galilee.

"And when on the earth I move again,
  And help the poor I see,
Ah, the song of the angels is deeper then,
  And heaven's more dear to Me!"

He bless'd me with His wounded hands,
  And He cover'd His spear-gash'd side;
And His face shone fair as He bless'd me there,
  When He carried me o'er the tide!

"COME, for my feast is spread,"
The Master softly said.
    Alack, I could but sigh,
    And send Him my sorrowing cry—
"Ah, Lord, I am with the dead!"

"Come, for my love will wait,"
He said, "till night is late."
    Nay, Lord, we have the will,
    But the House of the Sleepers is still,
And none unlatch the gate.

"Come, for day darkeneth!"—
And a breath like a rose's breath
    When dreams of Summer pass
    Stole through the listening grass,
And stirr'd the House of Death.

And, or ever we saw or knew,
Into our hearts it blew,
    And out of the grave's dank mould
    Our hidden lives unroll'd,
And He look'd us through and through.

False were we all, and shamed,
And we trembled to be named.

"Poor slaves of Sin," said He,
  "My pity sets you free!"
And His eyes like a cresset flamed.

O Thou, the Christ most true!
Thy love I never knew,
  Else had I loved Thee more,
  When the tides beat on life's shore,
And the skies of the world were blue!

WHERE ART THOU, CHRIST?

Where art Thou, Christ? Comest Thou back no
    more?
"Nay, I am with thee always. Open thou wide
    the door.

"Lo! I have longed and waited, out in the wind
    and rain.
Watch'd thee nursing thy sorrow, heard thee
    moaning thy pain."

Ah, let me go to Thee, Master! Poor is this house
    of mine.
Hold me, and guide me home where the lights I
    long for shine.

And the hearts that on earth were silenced wait
    in Thy heavenly place,
With Thy love like a robe around them, Thou
    Christ the King of grace!

IF ONLY——

Where I look on the line of the moorlands,
   And the heart beats free,
And the stars of midnight listen
   To the wide-blown cry of the sea,

I have bowed with my breaking sorrow
   Till it sobb'd in the shivering grass;
I have felt Thy shadow linger,
   I have heard Thy footsteps pass.

O come, Thou Christ of mercy,
   Who hast known the griefs of men.
I'd follow Thee where Thou'dst lead me,
   If only Thou'dst come again!

SUFFICIENT

Lord, I am weary, lonely, full of fear.
  "Hush, My beloved! My strong love is near!"

Father, I falter, failing in my place.
  "Hush, My beloved! Christ will give thee
    grace!"

Father, To-morrow daunts me, cold and grey.
  "Mine is To-morrow; conquer thou To-day!"

Father, the darkness deepens into night.
  "Fear not. Abide with Me. Thou shalt see
    light!"

Father, I die. . . . No more I see the sun.
  "Child of the dust, be strong. To-day thy
    work is done."

So be it, Lord. My fears aside I lay.
Help me to clear earth's dust from heaven's great
    doors to-day:
Then let the morrow bring me what it may.

THE JUDGMENT SEAT

"Where have you been, my brother,
    For I miss'd you from the street?"
"I have been away for a night and a day
    On the Lord God's judgment seat."

"Who would have thought it, brother,
    For the world's heart-breaking cry
Has arisen the same from sin and shame
    As when you said Good-bye!

"And what did you find, my brother,
    When your judging there was done?"
"Weeds in my garden, dust in my doors,
    And my roses dead in the sun.

"And the lesson I brought back with me,
    Like silence, from above,
That upon God's throne there is room alone
    For the Lord Whose heart is love."

THROUGH THE UNKNOWN

Give me a new book, Father,
  Let me sit a while at Thy feet;
Then let shadows or sorrows gather,
  Thy love will make them sweet.

Show me the new path winding
  Away through the unknown days;
Then let Joy or Grief come blinding,
  My heart will throb Thy praise.

Let Christ the Comrade guide me,
  Though the mist lies dark and lone.
May the starless mirk not hide me
  In the way I have not known.

Though the sharp-set flints should bleed me,
  Though I never a footstep see,
May the mystic pathway lead me
  Out of darkness, home to Thee.

NO MORE SEA

One sang of a world beyond,
    And he said, "There is no more sea!"
But a tideless heaven would be poor indeed
    To a Christ of Galilee!

For He loved the starlit deep,
    And the white waves on the shore;
And He dream'd of the fisher-boat's seaward
      sweep,
    By the Carpenter's cottage door.

And in heaven's vast home on high
    His heart cannot forget;
And He calls to His fishers to trawl and try
    With Love's great trailing net.

Peter and Andrew there,
    And the Galilean crew,
How they'd yearn till heaven grew dark with care
    For the wind-whipp'd stretch of blue.

O save the far-blown deep
    For the souls of the sea-born men;
Or leave us in pity, alone, to sleep,
    And dream of the drift again.

For to us, from our island homes,
    A heaven with no more sea,
A tideless day, would be poor and grey
    As to Christ of Galilee.

OUT OF THE DEPTHS

Ah, lift me from the dust,
Thou Love in Whom I trust,
  And make of my poor clay
    A vessel fit to bear Thy holy light,
  To guide to Thy sweet day
    Hearts that are blinded, groping through the
      night.

Then, Thy great purpose done,
And their calm heaven won,
  Quench me, and put me by,
    Somewhere beside Thee in Thy place above.
  Ah, it is not to die,
    To lose my light in Thy sweet morn of love!

Dust was I from the first,
And now, by sin accurst,
  Break me not in Thy wrath;
    Though even then I know 'twere very sweet
  To help to make Thy path,
    And bear the passing of Thy pierced feet!

Low was the door of shame
I enter'd when I came,
  And low the door I seek;
    And groping in the grasses I go hence.
  Stoop to me, Lord, and speak
    Thy words of love to bless my penitence.

And take me as I am,
Needing Thy pity's calm,
    Thy strength in all my fear.
    The comfort of Thy never-failing grace
Yearning I seek for here. . . .
    O shed on me the gladness of Thy face!

IN LOVE'S GARDEN

'Tis the world's sweet month of roses,
　And there's summer in the air,
But the chill is in my garden,
　And my trees are bare.

Is there aught for human sorrow
　But in silence to be laid
Where the lov'd are softly sleeping
　When the roses fade?

Come, Thou Shepherd, to my garden,
　And, though bare and bleak the place,
All my heart will glow, beholding
　Love's light on Thy face.

I BIND my heart this tide
  To the Galilean's side,
  To the wounds of Calvary,
  To the Christ Who died for me.

I bind my soul this day
  To the brother far away,
  And the brother near my hand,
  In this town, and in this land.

I bind my heart in thrall
  To the God, the Lord of all,
  To the God, the poor man's friend,
  And the Christ Whom He did send.

I bind myself to peace,
  To make strife and envy cease.
  God! knot Thou sure the cord
  Of my thraldom to my Lord.

ECCE HOMO!

O CHRIST! before Thy wondrous Cross,
   The glories of the world are dead,
And all earth's golden crowns are dross
   Before the thorns that gird Thy head.

We ebb and flow like ocean's tide——
   A shadowy drift of weary men:
Teach us the Love that for us died,
   And give our darkness joy again.

O wounded hands that played their part,
   That weeping mortals might be blest,
Touch ye, in love, my throbbing heart:
   Let there be pity, peace, and rest.

THE ANGELS' SONG

Thus the shepherds told it
  In the dawn of day . . .
Where their flocks were folded
  In the wilds they lay.

Some awake, some sleeping
  On the lone hillside;
Sudden, earthward sweeping,
  Song fell far and wide——

Like a soft rain flinging
  Love and joy o'er life,
Peace and Mercy bringing
  To a world of strife!

Never tongue has named them;
  They have pass'd away.
Night again has claimed them,
  Lost to us for aye!

Yet, ye hosts of angels,
  What would we tired men
Give to hear your singing
  Through the dark again!

Weary hearts are pining,
  Sick of sins and scars,
While above are shining
  Griefless, God's white stars.

Heavy lie the highways,
  Dim with dust and heat.
In what hidden byways
  Wait the Master's feet?

Earth is thrill'd with sobbing,—
  Crushed with shame and wrong.
O to hear the throbbing
  Of the heavenly song!

Could we hear it beating
  At Night's gloomy gate,
All our fears defeating,
  How our hearts would wait,

Till, o'er Hope's pale embers,
  Ere the dawn burn'd red,
Words the world remembers
  Clash'd their joy o'erhead!

O LET ME LOVE THEE

O LET me love Thee, Lord, who died
    For love of me.
Close clasp me to Thy wounded side,
    And keep me free
From sin and sorrow, self and shame,
And all that clouds Thy blessed name,
    Whate'er it be.

And help me, in this narrow place,
    Wherein I move,
To bear to saddened souls Thy grace,
    And ever prove
That love alone the path can trace
Which seeks the glory of Thy face,
    Thou King of love.

THE ASPEN'S SORROW

WHILE kindly slumber swathes the misty world,
 And all things sad are sleeping,
  What voice awakes,
  And sorrowing breaks
 The stillness with her weeping?

Silent the soul of Night
Lies, listening, with affright,
 Like a tired child awaking
  In wonder what the enfolding dark may
   be;
And lo, a deathless grief,
Seeking in tears relief,
  A murmur like the breathing of the sea,
 Lone, deep, heart-breaking.

Hush! 'tis the aspen trembling in the shade
 For Calvary's sorrow.
  Her anguished breast
  Can know no rest,
 Her night no morrow;
Ever the tide of her remorse comes sweeping,
 For Jesus weeping.

He toiled in Nazareth, waiting till His hour
 Struck through his heart, and bade Him
  cease His dreaming;

And, in the hills, or by the blue waves'
    gleaming,
He lingered, till their power
    His soul o'ershadowed, and a Voice He knew
        Called Him, and made Him answer, and
        He went,
        Into the hard world's passion, to be
        spent,
    Telling the vision true,
    The real behind the seeming.

All fair things loved Him. Streams and sounding
    seas,
Birds in the cloudland, shaking melodies
    Like softly falling rain,—
  The lilies in the long, lush, meadow grass,
  The whispering trees,
    The waves of shadow and of sheen that pass
    O'er hill and plain,
    Spoke to His Spirit, and the weary smiled,
    Out of their care beguiled,
      As He passed by;
  The dying turned to bless Him ere they slept,
    Nor feared to die;
And earth's sad outcasts crept
And sought His pity, and He looked, and wept
Above them, in their shame, about His feet:
    Till the deep wonder of a love like God
    Lighted the dust He trod,
And, like an old song sung in days long dead,

Ere Faith sank slain, and Hope lay withered,
Peace came again,
And drew to life sad women and tired men,
Crushed in Sin's trampled street.

But, on a day, when Hate of the world was king,
One that had walked beside Him, basely sold
His Lord for gold
    To base men's cruel will;
And they who bought,
Out of the woodlands green the graceful aspen
    sought,
And, from her body Christ's cross fashioning,
They nailed Him there upon the wind-swept
    hill.

And there His agonizings entered her,
And, for her doom, His pain
Her heart must stir,
    In daylight, starlight, sun, or shade, or rain.

Nor can she find relief
    Through all earth's years;
For ever sounds, across their gloom, her grief,
    With shuddering sighs, and sound of falling
        tears.

NOT WORTHY, LORD

I AM not worthy, Lord,
To bear the flaming sword
    Thy saints bear through all lands.
Mine but to pray and labour, and to wait,
Wondering beside Thy gate,
    With wounded hands:

Knowing Thy hands will pity my poor plight,
Stumbling through sin and night,
    By crag and thorn,—
To lift me, when all weariness is past,
And Love Divine stands victory-crowned at last,
    In Thy sweet morn.

CHRIST SLEEPING

I SAW Christ sleeping
  In the moorland bare.
Cold the winds were o'er Him sweeping,
  And the dew was on His hair.

And with sore sighing
  Did my heart nigh break;
For I heard the sad world crying,
  And I fear'd He would not wake.

Till dawn came golden,
  With a sweet surprise;
And His soul no more was holden,
  And the sleep fell from His eyes.

His glance did win me
  Where I linger'd lone—
Broke the pride of sin within me
  Like a lightning-riven stone.

Rose Christ up gladly
  In the moorland grey—
Heard the cities moaning sadly,
  And He swiftly walk'd away.

Often come I creeping
  From the streets and shore;
But in vain I search the moorland—
  Christ is sleeping there no more!

LOVE OUTCAST

Who knocks? . . . The sea is sobbing on the
    shore,
    And night is full of sorrow, as the wind
      Moans round my chamber door,
    Like some sad heart that may no shelter find.

I will not answer. Yet ah! knock again.
    I know who comes in darkness stranger-wise.
      No more . . . And though I fain
    Would ope, I dare not meet those sorrowing
    eyes

That in the darkness wait me just outside,—
    Silent,—amid the Night's forsaken cry
      And wail of Ocean's tide,
    For Love stands there whom I drove forth to
    die.

STREAMLET SINGING

Streamlet singing to the sea,
    Songs of gladness, songs of care,—
Thou art but a part of me.
    'Tis myself goes weeping there,
Through the dark along with thee.

In my heart the wild flowers grow,
    And the bonnie birdies sing,
And the winds of wonder blow,
    Sobbing, sorrowing, carolling,
And the stars within me glow.

Till the voice of bird and tree,
    And the gurgling waters gleaming,
And the deep song of the sea,
    And the moonlight's mystery streaming,
Make a world of God in me.

PENITENCE

Wonder of God, uplifting
  Souls that in darkness lie,
Here when the days go drifting
  Wilt Thou not pass me by—
  Sinful, ready to die?

Love in my heart was singing,
  And fair was the dawn of day,
The air and the earth were ringing
  With gladness—now far away—
  And now I dare not pray.

For I knew—and I know what beauty,
  Thou sett'st to dwell in my heart.
But I barred my door on Duty
  And I bade sweet Love depart.
  Now I know not where Thou art.

But Thou—wilt Thou find me, Father,
  Though the joy of my day is set,
Though the angels around Thee gather?
  Ah, I know Thou wilt not forget
  Me shamed, unclean—ah, save me, God,
    for Love's sake yet.

THE QUIET HOUR

EARTH waited long
 For the angels' song
To wake her from her sleeping;
 Though the blessed strain
 Rang o'er the plain
Where the poor their watch were keeping.

 The quiet hour
 Has still its power,
And its vision full of beauty:
 And God's own voice
 Speaks through earth's noise,
To the poor, in the path of duty.

 O watch and wait,
 For the hour grows late,
Sweet rest to your labours bringing:
 Lay sorrows by,
 For Love draws nigh,
And list to the angels singing!

THE WELL BESIDE THE GATE

Last night I was in Bethlehem.
  I had wander'd over the waves;
  But I long'd for a look at the moors again,
    And the old, quiet, grassy graves.

It was my heart's own Bethlehem,
  The ghost-place of my dreams,
Where the sea calls far among the glens,
  To the listening lochs and streams.

O quiet and still were the winding roads
  'Mong the rocky uplands steep;
And the broad tide swung a cradle croon
  Where the clachan lay asleep.

A hungering ache was in my soul,
  And a thirst no streams could sate;
And I thought of the Well of Bethlehem,
  That stood beside the gate.

By the mountain gate, where the road comes
    down,
  With its dusty tracks that led
The feet of the Seekers, aglow with hope,
  And the home-returning dead.

Last night I knelt by the mossy stone.
  I would drink of the well once more,

As I drank when the dreams of my life were gold,
    And the joys of life ran o'er.

Lo! 'twas as brackish as Dead Sea pools,
    Gross with the sand and clay.
The glamour and spell of the wayside well
    Were faded all away.

Was it my heart that the world had sour'd?
    Were these waters ever sweet?
Did the bluebells blink at the mossy brink
    That gurgled by my feet?

Ah, go not back to Bethlehem.
    Let it hold unchanged its part.
Keep the dream of the past while life shall last
    Unchanged within thy heart.

REST

HERE, where the city surges in its passion,
  Struggling and throbbing, through the morbid
    mist,
  Came a sweet vision to me ere I wist,—
A vision fair, transcending earthly fashion.

Methought a spirit led my feet away,
  To a great crag of silence, by a sea,
  That evermore kept moaning ceaselessly,
And ever, vainly, seemed for rest to pray.

As in a trance I stood, and then, at length,
  Out of the sobbing of the warring wave
  A voice arose, now low and hushed and grave,
Then swelled to heaven in wild despairing
    strength.

I turned me to my guide, and said, while tears
  Rushed to my lids, "Is there no rest on earth?
  Must all that from the chaos e'er had birth
Throb on for ever, tost by griefs and fears?"

He smiled a sweet reproach, and drew his palm
  Across mine eyes.—Before my 'wildered gaze
  Dropt into ocean the horizon haze,
And lo! I saw beyond, a land of calm.

With the blue heavens themselves, the hills
  seemed crowned.
  Sweet shadow wrapt the valleys of that land:
  And streams, like songlets, crossed the broad
    white sand,
And mingled with the sea's soft slumbrous sound.

He said, "Rest yonder lies—strife is forgot.
  That is the sea of Life whose billowy mass
  Thou must breast boldly if thou'dst hope to
    pass
To yon fair land, where turmoil troubleth not."

"Show me the way," I cried, "to yon blest land!"
  But lo! He vanished. As He passed, I saw
  A glory round His presence, and, with awe,
Thorn-wounded brow, and nail-imprinted hand!

THE COMRADE OF THE SOUL

Thou art sick, and thou art sad,
  Thou art blind and weak with sin,
And thy sorrow makes thee mad,
  But thy peace thou yet shalt win.

Thou hast left thy Father's halls
  For the desert, waste and wide,
And thy salt grief ceaseless falls,—
  Yet thou'lt reach thy Father's side.

For He watched thee all the while,
  Saw thee bleeding, faint and pale,
Drooping in the desert mile,
  Drifting, lost, without a sail.

And His love, with pitying haste,
  Sent me from beside His knees,—
Me, the Guide across the waste,
  Me, the Pilot of the seas.

Angels singing woke the morn
  When in Bethle'm I had birth,
But thy griefs with me were born,
  And I never knew thy mirth.

So I hold thee by thy hand,
  Till, beyond the gloomy gates,
I shall bring thee to that strand
  Where the griefless morrow waits.

CEASE FROM MAN

HEED not the voices sneering round you:
Follow the star that in darkness found you.

Scorn thou the scorn of the world's heart,
   grudging:
God is your King—let Him do the judging,

Till, when the day breaks over the sea,
He weighs what the worth of your work shall be.

GETHSEMANE

Go forth, alone, my Lord, to pray
   In dark Gethsemane's retreat.
Already sounds it, far away,
   The tread of Thy betrayer's feet.
"Judgment and death," Thy servants said,
   "Lord, we will brave them all for Thee!"—
Lo! now they sleep, with drooping head,
   And there, alone, they let Thee be.

Go forth, alone, my Lord, to pray.
   Yet O, afar off, on my face,
With eyes averted from the day,
   My Saviour, let me take my place.
In my Gethsemane of tears,
   O be Thou near to nerve my soul,
Though round me, like a host with spears,
   My doubts and dangers darkly roll.

Go forth, alone, my Lord, to pray;
   But let me say Thy words with Thee,
That I may learn the deathless way,—
   That I the radiant morn may see;
That, through the world's rebuke and scorn,
   To Thee my longing soul may rise;
That, when night merges into morn,
   I may be Thine in Paradise.

THE SOWERS

OUR eyes were dim with tears,
    As we flung the seed afar,
  For we knew how the rain and the wind and
      frost
Would follow the rich grain widely tost.—
Our hearts were filled with fears,
For we thought of vanished years,
    And the gate of Hope seemed firm and fast,
    and grey Death held the bar.

O many a day has fled,
    Days many, and brief, and long;
  By the gate of Hope sweet Faith was born,
  And we knew we should see a harvest morn,
When the hungry should be fed,
And the grain, from its dark low bed,
    Should rustle and gleam like garnered gold,
    and the world's heart beat with song.

Therefore we do not fear,
    Though the seed sleep under the sod;
  Toiling and struggling our souls keep true,
  And wait for the victory breaking through:
Knowing that, there or here,
Whether afar or near,
    One day the shadows shall drift apart, and
    the dawning come with God.

THE VOICE OF ONE CRYING

I HEARD a voice that rang through night and
    cried—
  "The dead is risen, and Jesus Christ is King!"
I looked aloft. The stars in heaven had died,
    And night hung overhead—a lifeless thing:
And still the voice rang on, "The dead is risen.
Empty the tomb, and rent in twain the prison."

O soul! I said. How can the dead arise?
    Have they not lain in darkness under earth,
With dust and darkness o'er their laughing eyes,
    And silence sealing up their lips of mirth?
They wake no more, who slumber in the grave.
Hush, O mad singer, hush, nor longer rave.

Lo! as I slept in silence of the night,
    Into my chamber a bright Presence stole,
Laid on my lids a finger-tip of light,
    Opened the dim perceptions of my soul.
Lo, it was Christ,—the cere-clothes round His feet,
Risen, my Lord, the King of Love, most sweet.

O lonely voice that sang aloud, when Night
    Hung dark and pall-like over all the skies.
Now know I well I heard Thy words aright,—
    Full well I know in truth the dead do rise.
And still about my gloom thy brave words ring,
For Jesus rose, and Jesus Christ is King.

RISEN WITH CHRIST

Touch the rock-door of my heart,
  Christ, dead for my sin!
Say, "Come—let us rise, and depart
  From the shadows within—

Out where the light of the stars
  Shines clear overhead;
Where the soul is free from its bars,
  And Sin lies dead."

And dead the old Shadow lies,
  That has chilled my breast;
Say to the sleepers, "Arise!"
  Lead them to rest!

BETHANY

THE lights are out in Bethany,
    Dust sleeps on the silent floor,
The laugh is hushed in Bethany,
    The song awakes no more.
For they've carried him forth to his bed of rest:
Roses and lilies above his breast.
    The love and the life of Bethany,
        The days of its joy are o'er.

We meet not now at Bethany:
    Its halls are weird and still.
We pass no more by Bethany,
    Nor pause along the hill:
For the homestead's gloom is a grief to see:
Ever the breeze wails lonesomely,
    And a dirge is borne by Bethany,
        On the breast of the sleepless rill.

The dead is gone from Bethany,
    Afar from our faltering ken:
No voice is stirred in Bethany,
    No living feet of men.
But shadows of dead men pause and sigh—
"Alas for life that love should die!"
    And the dust grows deep in Bethany
        Till Jesus come again.

LEAD ME, O GOD

Lead me, O God, through many a darkened room,
    And field of gloom,
        To where Thou art.
It is enough to know that Thou art near,
And through the praise of triumphing saints to
        hear
        The love-pulse of Thy heart.

So, when I wander, help me to Thy way,
And, in my battle-day,
        Weary and wavering, help me to be
        strong.
It is enough, if, when Thy kingdom come,
Though I be scarred, and battle-worn and dumb,
    I see Thy face,
        And, from some shadowed place,
        My silence floods with song.

THE WANDERING STREAM

"WHAUR are ye wanderin', windin' stream,
    Wi' the singin' heart within ye?
      Hae ye lost your road,
      And stachered abroad,
    Whaur the mists and the rain-draps blin'
      ye,—
      Till the waters' gleam
      Braks on your dream,
    And the sang ye are seekin' fin' ye?"

Speir nae questions. My airt's my ain.
    I gang whaur the music lead me,
      Whaur the sedges grow,
      And the wild flowers blow,
    And the weary cattle need me;
      And the hearts in pain
      For my springs are fain,
    And the bairns, like a braid beuk, read me.

What ken ye o' gudes or ills,
    Or the thochts that wi' God are springin'?
      Crookit or straight,
      Gae ye your gait,
    Whaur the dew or the tear-drap's clingin';
      Through ease or care,
      Through toil or prayer,
    Till ye hear God's angels singin'!

THE SHADOW OF THE CROSS

Here, 'mid the travail of our world's unrest,
   I laid me down to slumber in the dark,
In cavern'd hollow far in earth's sad breast,
   Remote from song of stream, or lay of lark;
Sleep on mine eyelids fell—my whole soul slept,
While, over all, her vigil midnight kept.

Sudden, upon the turning-hour of night,
   My heart stood still—my spirit slept no more;
The vault of heaven seemed glorified with light,
   A shadow swam in silence on the floor,
And through the throbbing night a murmur came,
Sweet as a dream of bells, that spoke my name.

I raised mine eyes, a-wonder-wide, to gaze,
   I could not bend them down to earth again,
Such vision met their question and amaze;
   For, high above the tribes of earth's tired men,
The Christ upon the Cross, in woful guise,
Stood, girt with glory, in the starless skies.

Still in the mid-hour of earth's joyless night
   I watch Him there, I cannot turn away,
His stirless Presence, shadowed 'gainst the light
   That girds Him round, awaiteth His own day,
And still, in awe, my wakened spirit hath
The shadow of Christ's Cross along its path.

HELP US, O GOD

Help us, O God, when day grows dark and
    clouded,
  And shadows sleep along the shore and hill,
And our belovèd, shrouded,
  Lie stark and still.

Help us, O God, when all our joys are fading.
  And all our dreams, our dearest and our best,
Look in our souls, upbraiding
  Our sin confest.

Help us, O God! What have we but our sorrow,
  That hushes gladness, walking by our side?
Hope scarce awaits the morrow
  Break o'er the tide.

Help us, for all else trembles, unavailing;
  Weak is our strongest, poor and sad our best.
Guide our frail shallop sailing
  Through storm, to rest.

THE MESSAGE

Sing and shimmer, wandering water,
　Through the meadows wide and free;
Sunshine gleaming through thy dreaming,
　Onward to the misty sea.

What the song within thy sorrow?
　Stay, my heart, and let me hear,—
"From the ocean to the ocean,
　All the journey, God is near!"

HYMN OF THE CHILDREN

THE tiny, twittering swallow
    That flits across the sky,
And round about the house-tops,
    And above the world so high,—
God guides it on its journeys,
    Afar o'er land and sea;
Then, if God so guide the swallow,
    Surely God will watch o'er me.

He gave me a father's kindness,
    He gave me a mother's love;
And many a gift I know not
    He sends me from above.
And Jesus, the Lord of heaven,
    Protects me night and day,
From the land where saints are singing—
    Happy land, so far away!

He'll guide me as I wander
    Through earth so great and wide;
Like a tender shepherd lead me,
    Ever lead me by His side;
For He loved the children fondly—
    He loves them still, I know,
On His knees He took them, smiling,
    And He bless'd them, long ago.

I long for the hand of Jesus
  To lead me through the night,
When the stars shall fade from heaven,
  And earth no more be bright.
I long for the kiss of Jesus,
  Me on His breast He'll lay,
In the hour He takes me to Him,
  To His bright land far away!

BY THE STILL WATERS

LEAD me, O Shepherd with the stricken side,
  And wounded palm,
    Beside Thy waters calm.

My soul is weary by the sorrowing tide,
  Of sin's dark sea;
    Lead me along with Thee.

Lift me afar from passion's fevered cry,
  And bid depart
    The pride that blinds my heart.

And let me learn, as at Thy feet I lie,
  With shame confest,
    Thy songs of quiet rest.

UNDER HIS FEET

Only to be as the dust that His wounded feet
   trod,
   Only to know and to hear
His love, like the deep-throbbing pulse in the
   bosom of God,
   Slaying my sorrow and fear.

Lord, I remember the sins and the shadows, and
   yet
   I remember the light of Thy face;
Let me but lie at Thy feet, and the black
   trembling horror forget,
   And only remember Thy grace.

Forgetting the darkness that walked with me all
   the way,
   The shadow that froze me to see;
Only remembering the joy of the breaking of day,
   When my soul found Thee!

GOING ON AFTER GOD

Stay, if you choose,
In the track where the crowds have trod,
Gaining what still they lose.
Following the star in its flight,
On through the gloom of the night,
Through the deep valleys, and over the height
I am going on, after God!

Stay, if you choose,
Where the clatter and sin never cease,
Seeking what still they refuse.
Far past life's passionate crying,
The selling of Fame and the buying,
Where the great silences softly are lying,
I seek for the palace of peace.

Stay, if you choose;
Yet Love and Life wait in the way,—
Alack, what beauty ye lose!
Peace, where before ye knew pain,
And Faith, where believing was vain,
And Hope that was dying, is quickened again,
As we pass to the joy of God's day.

Stay, if you choose;
Yet alack! low and chill as the sod
Is the life ye must use.

Ah, walk where the weary have need,
Bringing love where the crucified bleed:
To wake the dumb yearning to utterance and
    deed,
I am going on after God.

HOMEWARDS

I WILL arise and go, into the waning day.
They are waiting my feet returning,
And my heart with love is yearning
For the children far away.

All by myself, my own heart only,
Over the hills that lie
Grey, dark, and lonely,
Under the fading sky.

And I shall not feel it dreary,
Though the way be long;
And my feet shall not grow weary,
Though the night hold never a song.

For with me shall One go walking,—
I shall hear old voices talking,
And old yearnings whispering low.
So a long Good-bye.—
To live or die,
I will arise and go.

SUNSET

Hark! 'tis the evening bell. The sunset's glow
Laughs through the lattice—such a lonely laugh
As some sad warrior's, turning to his death,
Who feels his days of gladness are gone by,
And there alone, must bleed his life away,
By marge of moorland waters wrapt in mist.

So 'tis with us and life. The days pass sweet,
Till comes our sunset, and the lights are low,
And wan men turn wild faces to the wall,
And pass to death with laughter of despair.

O God, be Thou beside us, in that hour.
Sweet Jesus, be our Light to lead us home,
And teach us Sunset is not endless night,
But Thy great rest that fits us for Thy day.

HARVEST HYMN OF THE CHILDREN

Awake! 'tis the harvest morn:
   Sweet dew to the grass is clinging,
And among the yellow corn
   You may hear the reapers singing.
The birds are astir in the brake,
   And the joy grows grander, wider;
O awake from sleep!—awake
   To the praise of our Bread-Provider!

Thy harvest is on the hills,
   It gladdens the dreamy valleys,
It sleeps by the babbling rills,
   In nooks with the sun it dallies.
While the world of grown-up speech
   To Thee one anthem raises,
With the power which babes can reach
   We would lisp our Father's praises.

As Thy love aye guards the corn
   Slowly rising o'er the furrow,
So, ourselves, since we were born,
   Ever help from Thee must borrow,
For Thy harvest are we all,
   In the sun and shade we gather,
Till we hear the Reaper's call,
   And are taken to our Father.

So protect us, Father, still,
   In the broad, bright, sun-kiss'd meadows,

On the moorland—on the hill—
 In the glen's deep holy shadows;
And when comes Thy harvest day,
 And we lie in death's deep slumber,
In Thy bright land, far away,
 O our Father, do us number!

IN SHADOWLAND

On wings that waft me o'er the drowsy plain,
  Where poppy-wreathèd Slumber sits alone,
On silent-sweeping pinions I am borne past
    earthly pain,
  Past the sorrows, and the moan.

Gay Laughter, with the grape-stain on his lips,
  I leave all silent by the dolorous tide;
And Song that with high carollings could laugh
    at life's eclipse,
  At the shadow-limit died.

Strange, fleeting forms I meet with, in the mist—
  I feel the lone, low marsh's freezing breath,
And see who last on clammy brow and lip our
    lov'd hath kissed,
  The greater Slumber—Death.

His dark eyes gazed in depth of mine a space.—
  "Not yet!" He said, and turned aside, and
    sighed.
And day-beams broke: I stirred and spoke, with
    joy-dews o'er my face,
  That Christ had died!

AFTERMATH

Gather me, gather me, God,
  Into Thy harvest's glad singing,
    Home to Thy rest—
Up from the sod
  Where all my dreams have been springing,
    My poorest and best,
  With all that Thy reapers are bringing,
    Home in their breast.

Gather me, gather me, God,
  Leave me not, weary and dying,
    Lost and in pain,
Crushed in the clod,
  Like a forgotten thing lying
    Alone in the rain;
  Sad with the winds and their sighing,
    Hoping in vain.

Gather me, gather me, God,
  As grain in Thy hands do Thou take me,
    Sift me as wheat
Which Thine angels have trod;
  If there be pride in me, break me:
    Oh it were sweet
  To know that Thy sifting may make me
    Fit for Thy feet.

THE UNBAPTIZED

O LIST to the moan of the wind along the street.
    How it sighs by the eaves,
    And whirls the leaves
      Like listeners all surprised.
Ah no, it is only the homeless feet
      Of the little ones unbaptized.

They whimper and wail by the darkened door of
      home.
    With sorrow blind
    They cannot find
      A rest in all the world—
Like wind-blown birds of the driving foam,
      Along the darkness hurled.

O list to the cry of the wind along the street.
    How the mothers wake
    And fond hearts break
      With longings agonized,
For they hear the beat of the homeless feet
      Of their lost ones unbaptized.

Weeping like wearied pilgrims all the way,
    They drift by the door,
    And Love grows sore
      To rise and open free;
And lo, there is only the night-mist grey,
      And the sorrowing of the sea.

Ah, once I dreamed, in vision more than a dream,
>> That pity sweet
>> Drew me out to the street,
>>> For my heart was wrung with care,
And lo, in a dim, sad flickering gleam,
>> I saw the children there.

But a Shadow, with bleeding brow, thorn-
>>> garlanded,
>> With tenderest grace
>> Of love in His face,
>>> Though scarred from suffering sore,
In silence led the souls of the dead,
>> And angels walked before.

THE LARK'S SONG

My heart was heavy, and a hateful gloom
  Sank o'er my path, and quenched the sunny
      flowers;
And long I lingered in my lonely room,
    Through the dark hours.

I heard the watchman walk along the street:
  I heard the bells ring out chime after chime,
With merry voice, as if in glee to greet
    The flight of Time.

The varied sounds fell fainter through the town;
  Earth seemed to dream, and whisper in the
      dark:
Through the dim night no star sent earth-ward
    down
      Its trembling spark.

Thus hour by hour was numbered with the dead,
  Like silent weepers stealing sad away,
Till, through the clouds, a glory overhead
    Announced the day.

And sweeter than the chimes that rung on high,
  Richer than all the music ever born,
I heard the showers of song that filled the sky,
    And crowned the morn.

Now reck I not how dark soe'er the night,
   I know the cloak of darkness shall be riven,
I know the dawn shall shed its laughing light
      Through earth and heaven:

I know the sun's glad kiss shall wake the earth,
   And round the world a fairy garland fling,
And, like a spirit sprung to sudden birth,
      The lark shall sing!

THE DAY OF HIS COMING

I HEAR them again through the valley of sleep,
The songs of the Seraphs, through heaven as they
    sweep:
In silence of midnight they steal o'er mine ear,
And I know that the Day of His Coming is near.

Alone with the dead, in their dark, sleeping town,
I feel the sweet whispers of God stealing down;
Through the blue, throbbing darkness His voice
    ringeth clear,
And I dream that the Day of His Coming is near.

In slumber I lie with my feet to the East;
I shall wake when the Bridegroom comes on to
    the feast:
In His love folded closely I sleep without fear,
For I know that the Day of His Coming is near.

The green grass above me shall stir to His breath,
And His beauty shall pierce the dull garments of
    death,
And the heart filled with dust His glad summons
    shall hear,
And shall wake when the Day of His Coming is
    near.

The weary shall hear Him, the grieving rejoice,
The dead leap to life at the ring of His voice,

And midnight as dawn of the morning appear,
When the light of the Day of His Coming is near.

Enshrouded I slumber—the long ages roll,
But the songs of the Seraphs steal over my soul,
And I reck not the gloom of the woe-weighted
    year,
When I know that the Day of His Coming is near.

CURFEW BELLS

THE Sun goes dreamily to rest,
Slow stepping to the golden West.
  Dead sinks the long day's load of care,
  Amid the quiet fields, lone and bare,
      When Evening calls us home.

And darkness deepens as we go,
Until we greet the fireside's glow,
  Then close the dim grey shadows creep,
  And Pain and Sorrow sink to sleep,
      When Evening calls us home.

Lord! walk with us the darkening road,
And share with us our aching load.
  Life's cross of labour on our pride
  Grows light, if Thou art by our side,
      When Evening calls us home.

O let Thy love be standing by,
When bound in slumber's spell we lie,
  And be Thou near us when we wake,
  Where'er our morn of promise break,
      And lead us softly home.

IN THE DAY OF FAILURE

I HEAR the shout of the triumph
  From the hosts that are far ahead,
But I lie and die, O Father,
  'Mong the stricken and the dead.

And my heart grows big with yearning
  For the souls that pray for me;
And I leave no record written
  For the eyes that I love, to see.

But I look for a brave day's guerdon
  When Thy call shall stir the land
And I see the task Thou gavest,
  That falls from my failing hand,

Blest by Thy word of pity,
  Crowned with Thy word of love,
When I look to Thee in the dawning
  Slow breaking from above.

Thine is the day undying—
  Mine is the light that fails;
But the victory, Lord, is with Thee,
  Thy righteousness prevails.

And we who have fought Thy battles,
  O grant, when we awake,
We shall hear Thee speak, as we know Thee,
  All love—for Jesu's sake.

A PARABLE FOR CHURCHMEN

THE kirk wi' common fowk was fu',
The hymn was ower, the anthem through;
Wi' frozen feet and noses blue,
    We sat and listened;
And e'en, that tear-draps never knew,
    Wi' grim cauld glistened.

Ye moothed it oot wi' unco pooer,
For 'maist the best pairt o' an 'oor,—
Ye gied us't het, ye gied us't soor,
    Baith smile and froon;
Wi' bang that gart flee oot the stoor,
    Your neive cam' doon.

'Twas Lazarus at the rich man's gate,—
Ye're fond o' that baith ear' and late,—
A' sairs and sick, content to wait
    The dowg's ain share.
Ye gied us't at an awfu' rate,
    I do declare.

But, man, I'm thinkin' ye were wrang—
Mair solemn than a learnt-aff sang,
The words o' Him wha gaed amang
    The puir Himsel';
Ye didna need tae bawl and bang
    The truth tae tell.

For a' your days what hae ye dune
But suppit wi' a siller spune,
And ne'er on puir fowk lookit in
    E'en wi' a crust,
But lat them lie and steep in sin
    Until they rust.

Ye speak o' Lazarus wi' a tear,
Yet at the rich fowk's merry cheer
Ye're aft enough, and never near
    The humble bed,—
Never wi' solace stoop tae hear
    The last word said.

Oh! ye the Maister's name wha tak',
See that His truth ye dinna lack,
Ne'er say a thing and straightway walk
    A different roon',—
Your words like curses shall come back
    And crush ye doon!

AT THE DOOR

At the door of Thy love I lie;
   O rise and open to me,
Love that came hither to die
   That Thy Cross might set me free!

In a crumbling wherry I came,
   Over the lonesome deep;
I have crept by houses of shame,
   And graves where the weary sleep.

I know Thee what Thou art
   And what I might have been;
And I bring but an empty heart,
   Where Shame, like a knife, is keen.

Fill it again with song;
   Let Thy pity tune my voice,
That, through earth's sorrow and wrong,
   My soul may in Thee rejoice.

SAVE ME, MY FATHER

Save me, my Father,
  Sweetest name!
  From sin and shame
And fears that round me gather.

Open for me the door,
  And set me free
  To follow Thee,
My Master, walking ever on before.

Lead me, O God,
  Trusting, I know not where,
Save that it be where Christ has trod,
  And left Love's prints, like wayside lilies fair.

Till, in Thy place,
  Where sorrows never come,
  And pain is dumb,
I meet my loved, and see the beauty of Thy face.

THE CUP

WHAT holds the cup to drink?
What shadows at the brink
Shall fill my soul with fear,
Bitterness, failure, sorrow?
But ah! just think,—
God shall Himself draw near,
And the tears and sins of To-morrow
Ask me, Why did I shrink?
What shall I say,
When I feared, and let duty pass, and lost my soul
    To-day.

Thou Who didst die for me,
Whose face I sometimes see,
In darkness, and in dream,
Be near me when I fail;
My Saviour be,
From fleeting things that seem,
And the joys that on earth grow pale,
And hopes that, flickering, flee.

Upward, ever upward, O my Father, guide my
    going.
'Twill be sweet,
Though the path before my feet
Be in gloom, with mists of sorrow blowing
Through my life, from off the unknown sea—
Ah, God, to me,

'Twill be enough, to feel Thee by my side,
Till, darkness past,
I find Love waiting by the shimmering tide
To row me home at last!

BEYOND

O HERE, amid life's shifting sand,
  And earth's inglorious days,
I turn me to that mystic land,
  Behind the sunset haze.

O wondrous sweet Beyond,
  Where skies are ever blue—
Where rent no more is love's own bond,
  And all our dreams are true.

Here wearily the days go by,
  And never cometh rest,
Till side by side earth's children lie
  On their tired mother's breast.

But thine is never change,
  And never thine is night,
And never joys through sorrows range,
  But all is God's own light.

Here graves are waiting at our feet,
  And pain is ever near,
And faces fond, and voices sweet,
  Grow pale and still for fear.

But day undimmed is thine,
  And joy that knows no end,
And song that surges all divine,
  And friend that meets with friend.

O day of God's own deathless grace,
   Shine over me at last;
Sweet radiance of my Father's face,
   Be mine, ere life be past.

O wondrous sweet Beyond,
   Across the narrow stream,
Bring close the love of spirits fond,
   Dear country of my dream.

CHRISTMAS EVE

Christmas Eve in the City—
  Gaily the crowds go by.
With a trail of starry splendour
  The moon sails through the sky.

Soon, from the belfry ringing,
  The chimes will wake to tell
The old-world tale of the Baby
  Who conquered Death and Hell—

Who, born in lowly stable,
  Far off, and long ago,
Trod through this world, all lonely,
  Along His path of woe.

Scorned, buffeted, and weary,
  Outcast, sans hall or bed,
None saw the Beggar's kingship,
  Or the glory round His head.

Up by a narrow window,
  In a gable dark and high,
Where the city's Titan shoulder
  Looms black along the sky,

A woman waits and watches,
  A woman with heart of gold,
Though her gown be worn and tattered,
  As the God-man's was of old;

And, low in a corner lying,
　　A pale, pinched, delicate boy,
With deep, dark eyes of sadness.
　　O God, had they e'er known joy?

"Mother"—the woman started—
　　"This is the Christmas Eve.
Does the Christ-Child still come, ever,
　　And His halls of glory leave

"To come through the sky's far silence,
　　To the homes and the hearts of men,
To the souls that are warped and darkened,
　　And kiss them fair again?

"Blown hither from noisy streetways,
　　I hear the laugh and the song,
Like sounds that float from the darkness,
　　As a good ship sails along.

"There's a glow from the great, wide city.
　　It stretches into the sky,
For joy for the Man of Sorrows,
　　Who anguished even as I.

"O would He might come to our garret,
　　Here to this broken floor,
And kiss my lips from the fever,
　　And the agony, evermore!"

Surely the Christ-King heard him,
  Through the silvery-frosten night
He lay in his cot, in the darkness,
  Still, O still and white!

Surely the Christ-King kissed him,
  There, on his pauper bed,
For his soul had passed with the shadows;
  Only the clay lay dead.

LOVE'S SHADOW

I SAID the day was bright, and passing sweet,
   So still the land lay dreaming in the sun;
On through the hills, the singing seas to greet,
   The babbling streams in laughter seemed to run.

Quiet by my hearth I sat, and, in my heart,
   As in a chalice, brimm'd full joy untold;
Lo! as with thunder, sprang my dreams apart,
   And through my door fell shadow deep and
     cold.

Pain-pierced, I shuddering felt both sea and land,
   Touched as by Death's cold finger, sink forlorn.
Yet, lo! at threshold, Love, with outstretched
     hands,
   Stood,—on his face the gladness of the morn.

God's light behind Him smiled along the hills,
   O'er all, like music, hung the tremulous air,
So softlier now I follow where He wills,
   For Love's sweet shadow comforts everywhere.

CAROL OF THE MANGER BED

O THE shepherds lay watching their sheep on the
    plain
When the darkness was stirr'd by the Seraphim's
    strain—
"Now haste ye to Bethlehem," softly they said,
"To kneel to the Babe in the Manger's low bed!

"In weakness and want, and in poortith for thee,
He lies sleeping soft on His fair Mother's knee.
But angels are watching in sleep as He lies,
Till the morning of God wakes the dreams in His
    eyes!

"There are Kings of the Earth in their castles
    to-night.
And heroes renown'd for their valour in fight;
But none have the dream of the glory that's shed
O'er the Babe that now lies in the Manger's low
    bed!

"Ye Shepherds who wait by your flocks in the
    moor,
Go, bless Him Who gave, for the lost and the
    poor,
A Christ-child, the Saviour, to town and to glen,
Bringing glory to God, peace and goodwill to
    men!"

O they rose from their sleeping—they heard the
   glad strains,
They follow'd the song over Bethlehem's plains,
Till lo! in a Stable's poor state did they see
A sweet Babe asleep on His fair Mother's knee.

"Now art Thou the Saviour we're bidden to seek,
Thou Child poor and needy, forsaken and weak?"
But the angels of God gave Him light for a Crown,
Singing "Christ now is born in Bethlehem
   Town!"

Come, list to the Song of the Angels again—
"To God be the praise—peace and goodwill to
   men!"
Be it ours, Lord, to hear what the Angels have
   said,
And follow Thy light to the Manger's low Bed!

THE NEW SONG

I SAT in my soul's quiet chamber,
  And a music that pleased me made;
One stop, with a cry of conflict,
  Brave tones to my spirit played.

And I dreamed of days of battle,
  And my heart was proud and strong,
But the voice of consolation
  Ne'er entered into that song.

Till a Presence stole into the music,
  And as I sat awhile,
All silently leaned above me,
  And touched the keys with a smile.

'Twas as soft as if dews of sadness
  Were kissed away with tears;
'Twas as sweet as if voices silenced,
  Spoke again through forgotten years.

And I saw, as sweet peace sank round me,
  That it came from the world above.
'Twas the Master of Music playing
  His new sweet Stop of Love!

THE CHILDREN'S CAROL

Long ago, the angels, singing,
  Filled the shepherds with affright,
Through the skies at midnight bringing
  News that flooded earth with light,—
How, away in Bethl'em lowly,
  In a humble oxen-stall,
Lay the Baby, Christ the Holy,
  Who is King and Lord of all.

And the heavens were filled with gladness
  O'er the Babe that then was born,
Whose sweet Name removed all sadness
  From the souls of men forlorn;
And the stars all bright were shining
  Over stream and glen and hill;
Heaven and earth in peace entwining,
  Winds and waves were hush'd and still.

O my babes, be pure and holy,
  Ever keep your spirits true;
Christ the Lord was weak and lowly,
  He was once a child like you;
Him a baby's wants were given
  When to sad earth He came down,
From His glory high in heaven,
  Long ago to Bethl'em's town.

Now above the skies He reigneth,
  Girt with glory all around,

And his spirit ne'er disdaineth
Those who may His love have found.
When they cross death's darksome river,
They shall neither faint nor fall,
They shall reign with Christ forever,
Who is King and Lord of all!

IN THY MERCY'S DAY

Lord, in Thy mercy's day
   Remember me,
When like a dream away
   Pass earth and sea;

When I stand up alone,
   All heaven around;
And on Thy Judgment Throne
   Behold Thee crowned;

When all my sins appear
   About my feet,
And shadows that I fear
   My spirit meet,

Grant me, where sorrows cease,
   To see Thy face;
And, in Thy fields of peace,
   A lowliest place.

DE PROFUNDIS

O Thou, my Judge and King—
　My broken heart, my voiceless prayer,
　My poverty, and blind despair,
To Thee, O Christ, I bring.

O Thou, my Judge and King—
　My treason to Thy love most sweet,
　My pride that pierced Thy weary feet,
To Thee, O Christ, I bring.

O Thou, my Judge and King—
　My tearful hope, my faith's distress,
　For Thee to pardon and to bless,
To Thee, O Christ, I bring.

O Thou, my Judge and King—
　With no excuse, for Thou art just,
　My sins, that set me in the dust,
To Thee, O Christ, I bring.

O Thou, my Judge and King—
　My soul, from depths of my disgrace,
　To seek for mercy at Thy face,
To Thee, O Christ, I bring.

LOVE BIDING

TIME, take thy tears,
Thy threatenings and thy fears,
The joys thou offerest,
And what thou deemest best.
Whatever thou hast got
I need it not.
    While wide seas sever
        And while grey dawns break,
    I have what thou canst never
        Give nor take:

Love that abides
When perish all besides . . .
    Life, that when work is done,
        Draws close its door,
    And passes where there is no setting sun,
        In Christ, for evermore.

THE SONG

Lord, I would sing life's praises
    Like the lark as it leaps from its nest,
Rapt in Love's ecstasy, soaring
    With gladness fully confest:
But Thou giv'st me a song in the moonlight,
    With the thorn of grief in my breast.

I would sing like the throstle that's throbbing
    In the depth of the forest leaves:
But thou mak'st me a twittering swallow,
    Unrestful, about the eaves
Of the soul's dark house, where in sadness
    Love sits by herself and grieves.

Lord, give me a song of remembrance—
    The memory of Thy peace,
The roses of love that are faded,
    The sorrows that found release. . . .
To the melody of Thy mercies
    My singing should never cease!

IMMANUEL

Love, that made the thunder and the rain,
   And human fear and pain,

Speak to me, reminding my sad heart
   How very near Thou art,—

And flood the world's fear and passion's riot
   With Thine eternal quiet:

That I may know that Thou art God above,
   Who still dost give us love. . . .

If I come early, ere declining day,
   O meet me on my way:

Or late, betrayed by hampering despatch,
   Love's door be on the latch,—

And Thy sweet mercy, waiting as of old,
   To greet me to Thy fold.

BARTIMÆUS

I THOUGHT to give Thee pride,
   And strength and fire of youth,
As being what was best
   For Thee and life and truth.

And lo! I sank in shame,
   And what I deemed was most
To me, became as naught,
   And hush'd my proudest boast.

And so I bring Thee tears,
   A vexed heart, full of care,
Sorrow for empty years,
   A half-believing prayer;

Vows broken like cheap toys,
   Words fickle as the day . . .
O Love, show grace to me,
   A beggar, by Life's way.

IN OUR TIME

O LORD of love and life,
Close fast the door on strife,
That whisper'd ill may cease,
And human hearts find peace.

Protect Thy children, Lord,
From red oppression's sword,
Till in the lives of men
Joy finds her home again.

VIATICUM

Though starless dark sink over all
  I know no fear.
For Time is Thy servant and death Thy thrall,
  And Thou art ever near.

Though depths of silence cover me,
  And joy here dies,
In the flush of Thy morning Thy face I'll see,
  When dawn shall ope mine eyes.

I have no fee to pay my toll
  When forth I go.
Grey care is my comrade and sad my soul,
  And tired my feet and slow.

But the Home of love is open free,
  The gate stands wide.
And the lift of wings is given to me
  As I reach the further side.

MISERERE!

Be merciful, my God. These dying days
Carry me swiftly along life's shortening ways,
And with me all the failures I have known,—
The weaknesses that plucked me from my throne,
The stains upon my fingers and my heart,
The thing I hate, now grown of me a part.

Be merciful, my God. Ah, do not cast
My spirit from Thee, to the dark, at last.
Help me to conquest, lest I fall from Thee,
And miss the mighty Love that died for me.

AT THE DOOR

I AM the slave at the door.
　O rise and open to me,—
Lord, and King evermore,
　Who died to make me free.

Sad is my soul, and dark,—
　Dark is the lowering sky,
But I hear the seas and the angels singing
　Glory to God on high.

SAVIOUR AND COMRADE

HE saved me in the darkness when I fell
Close to the abyss of hell.

He walked the waters with me when the wave
Made cowards of the brave.

He leaned above me, when, with failing breath,
I stumbled near to death.

Shall He not walk these streets with all of you
If but your hearts be true;

And make within you, through grim sin with-
stood,
A fairer, manlier mood?

What though ye whimper, glad, for pain, to die?
He hears your feeblest cry;

And with your trembling palm in His pierced
hand,
Brings you again to land,

Out of the storm and drizzle, drift and foam,
Rejoicing, Home!

THE QUEST

Since Christ is risen
My trust
Is not in dust
That makes my soul's dark prison;
But, through the grave
Whose door
Can close no more
On those He came to save,
My hope goes seeking,
Nor fears,
Because it hears
The risen Jesus speaking;
And so divineth,
Undying,
Above life's crying,
His star of promise shineth.

LOVE'S OFFERING

Through the weeds and thorns that grow by the
    way
  Which leads to my home above,
I bear in my heart some flowers for God,
  That grew in the Garden of Love,—

A simple rose, and a lily or two,
  From the banks of quiet streams,
Some sky-colour'd bells from shadowy dells,
  And a little handful of dreams.

Not much in the big world's market-place
  Would they bring, if put to price;
But they gather their worth because they grew
  In the dust of sacrifice.

'Tis little at most we can bring to God,
  But we need not sit and fear:
A heartful of prayers, and a sorrow or two,
  To Him are always dear.

Nothing is empty, nothing is vain,
  If love be at its core.
He knows what life's bitterness fully can mean:
  And He waits for it at Love's door.

THE WAY

I FELL among the thieves
　And the many passed me by,—
Conning their speech or prayer,—
　And left me, stricken, to die.

O what was I but a dog,
　A thing beyond all hope,
For a name of ill was mine,
　And a woman had gone for a rope!

But one came down the way,
　A man of another church;
Look'd on me in my shame,
　Bleeding, left in the lurch.

He knew night was at hand,
　That the murdering thieves were near,
But he stay'd his step by me
　As one not born to fear.

He knelt by me in the mire:
　He laid aside his load;
And he cleans'd and dress'd my wounds
　With hands like the hands of God.

In his arms he lifted me,
　And his own load shoulder'd too.
"Don't fash, my friend,—you'll see
　I can carry it and you.

"It's as easy to carry two
    As it is to carry one.
Love laughs at loads," said he,
    "When the long day's darg is done."

He left me warm'd and fed,
    And my soul with thanks aflame:
Then away by the Road of Hate
    Without ever a word of his name.

Some fight for a printed book
    And some for a printed creed.
But the faith that lives is the faith that gives
    Love, warm for a brother's need.

THE CONTRITE HEART

I HAVE no precious ointment's sacrifice,
　　No alabaster box to bring to Thee——
For Thy great pity no rich answering price,
　　Nothing but scars for Him who died for me.

I can but fetch my grief from out the years,
　　Where life's broad field grew sin's harsh fruit
　　　　of pain;
Nought but a broken heart, and bitter tears
　　That fill my night with gusts of wintry rain.

My weary hands hang useless by my side,
　　And in my bosom sin and sorrow meet;
Out of the dark I crawl to Him who died,
　　And, through my weeping, kiss His wounded
　　　　feet.

Hast Thou a word for me? Ah, let me hear
　　The victory-whisper, full of sweet release——
"Soul, stricken sore, God's love casts out thy
　　　　fear.
　　Shake off thy sin, and enter into peace."

LOVE'S PASTORAL

THE Shepherd of Love is our Master dear:
　　And, whithersoe'er we roam,
From hills remote or from moorlands near
　　He gathers us softly home.

O many of hue and foolish we are,
　　And the range of His pasture's wide,
Where the peak is grey 'gainst the misty star,
　　Or the cliff broods o'er the tide.

O'er the water-meads His Presence goes,
　　And heart-deep through the flood:
His own He knows, for, when Morn arose,
　　They were mark'd by His own red blood.

His feet are pierced with the flint and thorn,
　　But never a step they lag
In His quest for the lost, or the lamb new-born,
　　Or the ewe that wails from the quag.

In the Valley of Dread we unshrinking wait,
　　Where Death's black shadows sleep,
For His hands that were scarr'd at Love's low
　　　gate
　　Shall ever us safely keep.

Though lost a while we huddle in fear,
　　Or wide through darkness roam,
With a cross for His crook He draws us near,
　　And gathers us softly home.

PEACE

Peace. . . .
From sorrow and sin release:
Where Love that has gone ahead
By the dark road of the dead
Wearies and longs and waits;
Till our futile searchings cease,
And, beyond the swinging gates
Of alternate Day and Night,
The song that we have lost,
And the joy that Sorrow tost,
Like a pebble, behind her here,
We find, past pain and fear,
In the wonder of deathless light. . . .

Rest. . . .
O Jesus ever-blest,
Draw us where we may find it
Folded within Thy breast.

THE GIFT

No treasure-troves of Art
    Within my offerings be:
Only a contrite heart
    That longs for peace with Thee.

A bunch of broken prayers,
    That once as flowers were sweet,
I bring, with hopes and cares,
    To lay them at Thy feet.

Thou readst life's scrabbled line,
    Thou knowest what is best. . . .
Lord, teach me to be Thine,
    That, serving, I find rest.

CHRIST WITH US

I DO not shrink from Death's low narrow door
Since He has passed before.

All ways by which His shining footsteps lead
Are ways to life indeed.

In day and dark my soul can know no fear
Since He is ever near.

And from His cross the word of victory
He gives with power to me.

Therefore o'er misty pass and starless ford
I follow with my Lord,

Till dawn shall scatter in transfigured light
The shadows of my night.

SPRING-SONG

God made my heart a garden of roses,
    Sweet and fair, with wild birds singing;
Soft as a dream when daylight closes
    And far-off evening bells are ringing.

But Winter came, amid Summer's gladness,
    Withered the rose-leaves, left them lying,
Dead things, touched by tenderest sadness;
    And song was turned to regret and sighing.

Lo! as I lay in my ruined garden,
    Came Love, still as the morning breaking,
Laid on my brow a kiss of pardon,
    And joy awoke like a lily's waking.

Stirred my soul, with a song of wonder——
    Laughed and leapt with a glad behaviour;
For not with winter, nor rain, nor thunder,
    But sweet as the springtime came my
      Saviour.

LOVE'S JEWEL

The moss-girt well in the depths of the moorland
    Clasps in its heart a shining star,
Like a jewel dropt from Night's own bosom,
    As she stoops to drink, from skies afar.

So when I lay in grief forgotten——
    Sorrow's shadow in gloom above——
Lo! from her breast, as she bent to whisper,
    Into my pain fell God's own love.

There, the deeper the darkness gathers,
    Brighter its wondrous glories wake;
Like the star in the heart of the well it lingers,
    Shining clear till morn shall break.

FAITH

Though the field of my heart be bare as a wind-
  swept plain,
Void of relief of tears, as a desert that knows no
  rain,
Yet still shall my faith keep ward, and my hope
  beat on
Till the love of my God speaks to me when Night's
  long shadow is gone.

Though my grief have for lullaby only the sob of
  the sea,
And the withering salt of the spindrift be blown
  over Love and me——
Though my feet limp lame, sore-pierced by the
  wilderness thorn,
I shall wait through the dark till I see God's
  waking promise of morn.

For the pity of God comes nearer the further I feel
From His thought, while above me the deep vast
  Silences reel,
Till, desolate, naked, with scarcely a pulse in my
  breast,
Love, wounded in seeking me, finds me, and,
  stooping, lifts me to rest.

There's a dove on the Cross sits brooding, and
  saying to me——

"Love that is stricken for others alone can be
  free;
Love that is crucified findeth the peace behind
  strife——
Giving is living, losing is winning, and Death
  holds the secret of Life."

RAGS AND TATTERS

Rags and tatters at best
Is the garment of my soul,
Torn in my wild unrest
By passions past control.
And the clay of my body rent
By the thorns thro' which I climb,
Up to eternity's quiet
Out of the storms of Time.

Rags and tatters at best——
But what are they unto Thee,
Since through my body's shame
Thy love my heart can see?
And Thy pity wades the stream,
Heeding not storm or foam.
With the husks of the swine-troughs on me,
Thou bringest me, broken, home.

Rags and tatters at best.
But my heart has still within,
Like the sigh of the sea in a shell,
Heaven's echo, unhusht by sin.
And a light like a mother's love
Has followed me all the way,
Till Thou meet'st me there, by the ford,
In the shimmer of breaking day.

Rags and tatters at best,
All I can bring to Thee,

Where jewels and gold and fame
Like ashes and dust must be.
Thou clothest my soul with love.
Thou fannest the dying flame;
And sett'st in the blood of the Cross,
On me, my Saviour's Name.

THE OPEN DOOR

THE Master stands at the table-end,
  And the lights shine far within,
"Let not the door be shut," says He,
  "Ere the bairns Love's shelter win.

"The night is dark, and the way is steep,
  And the wind is snell and cold;
Alack, for the lambs that are not safe
  In the bield of the moorland fold!

"Let a candle at every window shine,
  And the light stream from the door,
Lest the prodigal, last, from the swine-troughs
      come,
  Seeking his home once more."

And a hush on those at the table dwells,
  And the songs to silence fall,
When they think how the heart that on Calvary
      broke
  Is the sheltering home of all. . . .

Wait for us, Lord, when the darkening comes,
  For we oft are weary and lame,
And many a foot that was swift in flight,
  Lingers a while—for shame!

THE SLEEPERS

As the world goes rolling onward
    The sleepers turn and say,
"Are you keeping the old dream stainless
    That was ours in the long-dead day

"When beside the Cross of the Saviour
    We held our vigil tryst,
And welcomed the child God gave us
    As another man for Christ!——

"Sometimes the face of the mother,
    Grew wan with the fireside task,
And the daily bread that we longed for
    We scarcely dared to ask.

"But we went to our graves with gladness,
    In lowly hope and trust
That a richer day and nobler
    Should dawn above our dust.

"Ye that were born of travail,
    What we gave you, faithful keep,
Lest our tired hearts ache to awaking,
    And mourn in their place of sleep."

WAYFARING

God's love beneath me,
God's peace about me,
God's grace within me,
    Through daylight or dark,
Christ's promise walking,
Ever my Companion,
Still keeping burning
    Faith's feeblest spark!

So, as His pilgrim,
Often foot-weary,
Often with sorrow
    Stumbling and blind,
Through the grey dawning
And the dim darkening,
I still go forward,
    Love's peace to find.

THE CONSOLATION

I HAVE only a little candle,
  That was lighted at Thy word;
And my heart in my breast beats feebly,
  Like the wing of a fluttering bird.

And the way is sometimes dreary,
  Though glimpses break between;
And the dark blots out remembrance
  Of the glories that have been:

And the memories of Thy goodness
  Are wiped out by my tears;
And the strength of many a promise
  Forgotten by my fears.

Yet this abides to lift me,
  In the known and the unknown——
Thou didst not give me Jesus,
  To let me die alone.

CHRIST'S WAY

WHEN all the stars were lost in the leaden sky
I saw a shining Presence passing by,
And followed Him to see
Whither His way might be.

He climb'd the dark, and found the dying there,
And some that once were fair,
Loving and loved, ere sorrow of the years,
And pain of gloomy days, and bitter tears,
And poverty, had scored their furrows deep,
And Care had murder'd Sleep,
In their sad loneliness, where no foot came,
Since men forgot their name.

He touch'd them: and His contact brought them
    peace.
Care lost its fret, and anguish found release. . . .
So simple was it, yet divinely great:
And, for His sake, I learn'd 'twas mad to wait
Till the great Opportunity came past,
Radiant, with splendour vast,
Richer than ever o'er the broad earth shone,
All the bells ringing,
All the glad hosts singing,
And the wide-waken'd world all looking on,
While Christ Himself still sought the quiet way,
Changing men's night to day,
Hushing their pain and fear——

Unseen, by some chance heart lingering
    near——
And bearing to the souls in bitter need
Eternity, within Love's simplest creed.

HAGAR

My God, I perish! And no soaring cry
    To reach high heaven, can break from my
       parch'd lips.
    Yet here, on desert verge of life's eclipse,
Have pity.—Do not let my darling die!
Take *me:* my dusty hopes are all blown dry.
    My heart's pulse, like a perishing flicker,
       dips
    Into oblivion, and my fancy slips
Down the steep way, to madness by and by. . . .

Dimly I see my boy, through my despair,
    Less than a shadow's glimmer, by the brink
Of the great darkness—his bright shining hair
Beyond my touch. Of life give him my share——
    My heart a well from which his life shall
       drink
Red life again—Love like an angel there!

Down on thy face, by sudden thunder smote——
    Choked with the common dust that peasant
        feet
    Fleeing before thy rage, through noon-day
        heat
And frosty starlight, spurn'd into thy throat——
Till thy proud heart shall hear, with strange
      surprise,
    "O seeker, who, now soul-sick, canst not see—
    O weak strong man, My Cross has need of
      thee,
When Faith, pain-born, shall open wide thine
      eyes!"

Lord, I am blinded. In my mouth is dust——
    My heart slain with the storm of passionate
      years;
    Love, blinded, struggling in a sea of tears:
Yet still, dead on the clay, my soul shall trust
    This night to know Thy strong grace raising
      me,
    And dawn be stirr'd by my song praising
      Thee!

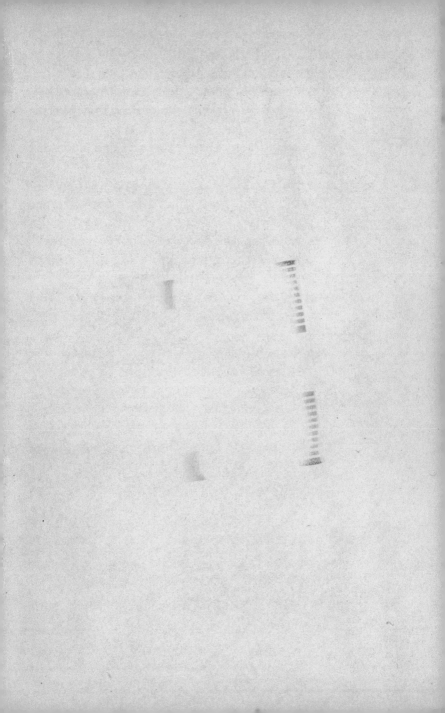